What It Wasn't

Books by Laura Kasischke

Poetry:

Wild Brides
Housekeeping in a Dream
Fire & Flower
What It Wasn't

Fiction:

Suspicious River
White Bird in a Blizzard
The Life Before Her Eyes

What It Wasn't

poems by
Laura Kasischke

Carnegie Mellon University Press
Pittsburgh 2002

Acknowledgments

Grateful acknowledgment is made to the editors of the following magazines in which some of these poems were first published:
Crazyhorse, *The Georgia Review*, *Green Mountains Review*, *The Indiana Review*, *Laurel Review*, *The Michigan Quarterly Review*, *The Missouri Review*, *Prairie Schooner*, *The Seneca Review*, *Willow Springs*, and *Witness*.

A Creative Writing Fellowship from the National Endowment for the Arts supported the writing of these poems.

The publication of this book is supported by a grant from the Pennsylvania Council on the Arts.

Library of Congress Control Number 97-76754
ISBN 0-88748-274-0 Pbk.
Copyright © 2002 by Laura Kasischke
All rights reserved
Printed and bound in the United States of America

10 9 8 7 6 5 4 3 2 1

PENNSYLVANIA
COUNCIL
ON THE

ARTS

Contents

One

Two

Three

for my dad, Ed

One

_____

I saw a body lying on the earth: which body showed heavy
and fearful and without shape and form, as if it were a swilge
in a stinking myre. And suddenly out of this body sprung a
full fair creature . . . shapen and formed, swift and lively, and
whiter than the lily, which swiftly glided up into heaven.
Julian of Norwich

Weak and dainty stitching will unravel
and shorten the life of the girdle. . .
Intimate Apparel magazine

MORNING

The August air has turned to blurred fur, all
flesh, paste, sponge, sprawled

wool on the humid hills. When

she puts the girdle on, there is the sound

of panting sheep, the sound

of sloppy, tropical fruit sloshing warm
and milky juice
beneath its skin.

COCKTAIL WAITRESS

Things change, but those days
my tray was always full

of damp blue veils, amazing

scarves of waste things washed
up gasping between the waves
as I ran into the future with them, the way

a child might run toward her mother
with wet hair like weeds
sopping in her hands
one morning at the beach. I still believed

the day would come
when I would bump straight into love
in a barroom, like
a businessman with wings. Later

I'd loosen his red noose
in a mildewed room
of the Holiday Inn, un-
button his stiff shirt

and there those wings would be, soft
and alive, two

wet white hens, cool
or clammy
under my hands. Half

skin, half
tissue paper smelling
like fresh and restless paste. They'd

tense and tremble
when I touched them, stunted

gulls with nowhere
to go, while my
fish-net stockings, strung
up, dripped
above the tub. But my

father called my roommates
the False Hope Club. Five
ephemeral station wagons idling, five
lilac blossoms browning

on the sidewalk, five
unsolved murders just
waiting to occur. We

lounged around in lipstick while the sky
rippled its
blue metallic dime-store slip outside, while

the heiress starved to death below us, and the thin
blondes above us made a feast
of water every night
by their TV. Once
we found a life-sized plastic doll

strung up behind our dumpster, like
a sacrifice to nothing, a dagger

through her heart, and down the block

a muddy set of women's
underwear was found
beneath some cardboard in a barn. My

father thought it was a warning
from our landlord, but I
still believed in miracles
and spirits of every kind, believed
one day I'd find a man who'd pant
and struggle

in a victory garden—mine—
snagged in vegetation, coiled

vines around his wrists. His
lush hair would be bleached
green, and there might even be

pumpkins swollen like awful
god-heads at his feet, or
overgrown suns—while my

figment fell and rose around him, a foil
screen, while my

melancholy figment
sipped a margarita

and filed her fingernails to speartips

in the future by his pool.

SECOND WIFE

August

Isn't she the one who comes to cover
the furniture in the Queen's cottage
with sheets when summer's done? (The

love seat, the bassinet, the blood-
stained rug.)

———————

Persephone

I was just his rib, his first wife says.
I cared for him. I slept with him. Did I have a choice? The way

the other women back away from Hades' wife in hell. She's

smiling in a bridal gown, and everyone knows her name.

———————

Saints

Always the beautiful bitter lives of the female saints, like

Domenica of Paradise, who lived
for twenty years with no

food except Communion. She

was said to have diffused a cool, celestial French perfume, but

seeing her in a pretty hat, her husband saw Jesus bleeding
instead. *Silly,* my best friend says, *Don't you know a man's*

first wife is always
Domenica of Paradise?

_____

The Neighbor's Husband

He steps one morning out of a cloud

of blue lawn-mower smoke. Ghost

and fox, with no shirt on. Leaves

have fallen like a golden

road from this house to his feet. Although

we've never met, his

wife's heart is full of my broken teeth.

DRINK ME

There's blue juice and usually
someone who'll squeeze it for you

from coma and plums and the fire you set
in a circle around
your own house

to keep the other fires out: It says

DRINK ME on the bottle, and when I do
I shrink and shrink, until
I could slip into

the TV glass, until my body could be carried without trouble
on the backs of two green bees, who

bump the invisible windows, or
zig-zag all day droning
over the rotten apples, the sugar cubes, the marigolds, with their
little fusty faces of grief. The air

smells ruined, bruised, fermented—sweet
as an orchard trampled
by God's big feet—while

the poison moons of Jupiter drag
the milkweed up and out
of its sticky sleep: Even

the goats who drink
the juice of this fruit grow
giddy and open-hearted, struggle

up to walk
on two feet
as human beings—until

they grow too fat

or tired, get mean, and gnash at one another
with cold, pink teeth. *Dear*

Mom I write home fondly

on the back of a postcard
of a frozen ocean *I*
thought I was done for a while forever

with the drinking, the drugs
and the men in leather. She

writes back *We*

know exactly what you mean. Usually
it's summer here in heaven
and the goats dance stiffly
all night with the girls, and though

the ballroom smells like roses, we always know

a tiny corpse rots under the floor.

CHILDHOOD VISIONS OF BEAUTIFUL WOMEN

They steal across the swamps
with bare feet
and green wings, not

dead, and not asleep, not
starfish, earthworm, fern—singing

Ivy growing on a stone,
Ivy growing on the earth,
Ivy growing on a stone on earth.

Scummed and purring, the swamps
are full of motherwort
and loosestrife

as they always were, while

back home, another woman wavers
in the kitchen's hallowed light, wearing

slippers in the middle
of the night. She

sings a song from far away—a song
from somewhere in between

grace
and the strange veiled rays
of the microwave—

Lichen growing on a birch,
Lichen growing on a church,
Lichen growing on the Virgin's marble robes.

RECOLLECTION

*During one of Wilder Penfield's operations, the right
temporal lobe of a woman was exposed and electrically
stimulated. The woman was fully conscious and
described her sensations. The recollection of a mother
calling her child was evoked, and that of a carnival.*

I was that mother one dust gray drunk
and ugly summer. I had

a picket fence   a violent husband   several
housewife friends with wine. At night

the carnival lit up a swollen
lip of distant sky   like
electric teeth on every side
of a dark dry tongue. It was

as if the child's name I called that night could scorch an orchid

or an onion
out of conscious
or unconscious earth   all
white light and lightbulb sprouting
tangled arms underground. Summer

was green
with green and pumping blood. Another

*woman's un-
remembered memory: All*

*that time, that's
all I was.* So

many years passed by her   stiff
as dreaming cows   while I

20

just turned to some-
thing glimpsed once
on a long dull drive through dust. But

that's the drive we all make one time

into the temporal center
of our own lost lives. *It was*

summer in the cornfield in the back seat of a dark car
as it sifted the smell
of soft rot   old

blankets soaked in fever sweat tossed
across our dreams. There

might have been cold
steam and change all spring

writhing like orchid
bulbs under her feet   the way

a vivid high school girl-
friend's un-
remembered maiden name might
swim to the murky

surface of the pond
on a rainy summer day. *Amnesia*

Paramnesia, Oblivescence, Fugue.

And another woman's life simply rises

from the right temporal lobe
of the open mind   moist

and encephalous as

some cool fish eye silver-spooned
out of a thin, gray soup.

Maggie, Mary Gail, Sweetheart come back: Witness

the strange kind wildness
of the brain   how

it will always open
its hungry mouth
one last time
to let the children out.

ANDY'S LANES & LOUNGE

On the night of the miracle cure.
On the evening of the electric chair

I am twirling on a barstool. Some-
one shouts STRIKE. A girl
shrieks. There's
waste and loneliness in public places, and the moon

hangs candy-red above
the watery world where
the terrorists have just discovered
the weapon that will kill us

all—a handful
of nightfall,
tucked in a bowling ball. There

will be squealing when it shreds us, and
the moon tonight is red as something

too sweet and full of female screams to eat.

———————————

On the night of the miracle cure.
On the evening of the electric chair

the man they execute lives—though
his white hair turns dove gray, though
his red hair smokes. And

the old lady they've
left naked and embalmed on a table, licks
her fingertips, which
still taste like flute, stainless

steel, sugarwater sweet as youth. *God*

I've never been less hopeless

and the bitters have never tasted
more like kisses, and

the maraschino cherry is so syrupy and bright
I have to hold it in my mouth and close my eyes
before I bite.

WOMAN IN A GIRDLE

Overgrown Garden

Afternoon wilts, the way
lungwort withers in hot weather, its

silver-spotted leaves gone
soggy and tubercular
sucking summer out of the ground.

———————————

Lazy Susan

The cat's tail sweeps the floor
while the dishes are washed

by the dirt. Now
all over the suburb
she can hear

the sweaty, stucco walls
of the human houses breathe

like cheese, and she

remembers seeing
the World's Smallest Horse
at the Lubbock County Fair, circling

its own shit
at one end
of a big pen. In its

small saddle, it

was so, so small.

———————————

Nap

The shepherd on the hillside
cannot keep the flock together.
The sun's been boiled to something pale

and flaccid as a dumpling. The shepherd

stumbles among them, but there
is so much yeasty light, he
can no longer tell

the sheep from the sky, which hangs
above the world, a woolly scarf.

———————————

Dinner

How skinny the Cornish hen
appears in the oven.
A plucked, baked, feminine
fist. Meal

for a prisoner
in a wide prison cell, bald
mouse in the lion's cage, while dusk

wraps itself around her—
a loose, blue cave.

———————

Dancing

All night the mockingbird sings
with its breast pressed against
a thorn, the way

the woman in a girdle dances
against a man
while twilight stings the sharp

and silver points of petals to the trees.

WHAT IT WASN'T

On January 1, 1976, Tracey Lawson, 11, and her cousin
were playing in a backyard five miles south of Harlingen,
Texas. As they looked out on a plowed field beyond the yard,
they saw a black bird of extraordinary size: over five feet tall.
Its wings were folded around its body, and the bird was
staring at the girls through large, dark red eyes. Its head was
bald, and it had a beak at least six inches long.

It wasn't night: We
knew everything there was to know
already about night, how

night is a small wool cake
of rodent bones, how

an owl can choke it up like
wisdom, or a tooth. We

were virgins, still, and cousins

so it wasn't about sex.
And it also wasn't death, like

the handfuls
of jackdaws
that every winter tossed themselves

down the hopeless chimney, head-
long into the cozy
hell of our wood stove. Even

the Stealth Bomber
would certainly have made
a dark new wind
with its bat wings. But this

didn't whistle

and it wasn't maimed. It wasn't

Mary, or the Air Force, or your brother Jim. Too

young yet to want
the government's attention
or the sympathy of cops, we

weren't mad, and we'd
never heard

about the netherworld, worm-
wood, pharmaceuticals, vermouth. This

wasn't the realm
of darkened sun, or
the unanticipated outcome
of sublimated lust, and we

were not the only ones: Two

men in Brownsville saw it
first, saw it
settle on a patio near a cooler

of brand new beers. This
thing certainly

was not no neighbor's pet, this
ugly, tarred & feathered angel. They

claimed it lunged

but didn't bite, that
it was not a Jungian symbol
of any type, not

even a symbol
of the dangerous action
of instincts upon
the drunken man. It never

crossed their minds
to shoot, or throw a rock, and only

three hours later it had winged
its way to us. And no

it was no whistler, I'll
grant it that, or
a wheezer, and, indeed, it did

not try to bite. Though,

after that,
the vacant valley, it
looked more vacant
than it ever had:

Clearly
a symptom
of dissolution, that

restless, indeterminate, ab-

straction of discontent. To some
it comes as tedium, a tepid
Calgon tub of tedium, the yuppie

flu, the dull dawn you wonder whether
you ever loved your husband, why
you ever moved to the suburb—but

we were only children, and to us

this thing occurred early, as
a man-sized bird. It

didn't smell, but
if it smelled at all it would have smelled
like useless, fashion boots. It *was*

sullen I'll admit, and always
a little drunk by supper, but

it never shattered families

or ended in divorce. It never
abused the power
it never wanted to have. It never

murdered, packed, or moved. Whatever
it was, it was

never what it was, not
even a shadow
of its former bird. Just

the sudden knowledge that
we'd been children once,

full of futures, and

we no longer were.

Two

My mother is very strange; if I bring her flowers, she says she does
not want them; if I bring her cherries, she will not take them, and
if I then ask her what she desires, she replies: "I desire thy heart, for
I live on hearts."
Joseph of Copertino

"A few years ago, if I had a gray outfit, I would go and buy a gray
bra and gray girdle. But today, I don't know. . ."
woman quoted in *Intimate Apparel* magazine

MY HEART

When August was finally done, his
wife never mailed the dark
card to me that said, "Hon

he's all yours now, good
luck and happy Labor Day," and still
I *loved* that man, the way

magnolias go
sloppy and wet as pneumonia
on front lawns when summer's over, the way

a cool moon might appear on a bright September afternoon
to the naked eye to be
just a blind blue infant face

hovering in space. Those
human trees: Listen
to them wheeze all night in sleep while

the washing machine churns blood
and whiskey out of your sheets. I
loved that man, whatever that means.

Whatever you need, I thought.
Whatever you eat. GOTCHA
he wrote one morning

in red pen above my breast. Bull's-eye
where my heart was, and the earth
bobbed a bit

on the little string that holds it
over a whoosh of air
and emptiness, the way

when I was a child a magician pulled
a long silk scarf
from my ear. I could hear

red wind when it passed
out of me into his hands. All
the other children at this party

gasped, but I
knew where he'd gotten it from, and felt
my heart spin in me like a sparking

toy when he was done.

BANSHEE

But it's animal, not spirit, wailing
out there. Coyote, wild dog—these
ordinary creatures of the world

are everywhere. Some nights

they stalk our neighbor's sheep. Some afternoons
I've seen them slip
into their lean shadows and disappear between

the shadows of the trees. It is

a warm night, window open, the end
of a century in which
the moon became a place to go, wandering

fogged and crescent, a long

canine tooth in the sky. Someone's

poodle wails as it wails, imagining
she's one of those wild cousins tonight, pink

ribbon between her ears, blood
on her pink tongue. And

above the howling, another
song—bleating? piercing? screaming? It goes on and on. One

shrill note like a shudder. It

tapers off, begins again. Treble. Sweaty. Terrible. Until it stops, then starts, and I

go to the kitchen for a glass of water. It is
too awful. It is

our house that old woman wails about.

LOST MEMORY, SUBURBIA

June. A woolly wind. A face of light on the thunderhead swimming
along the horizon like a Sphinx. The riddle

is unsolvable. It resembles

the sky. Amnesia

is green. Memory, blue: It's
like whatever it is that tiptoes through

a garden and makes
Victorian lace

of bean leaves overnight. It leaves

ragged holes behind, irregular
and absent, an intricate pattern of losses, which passes on, infinite,
            into

oblivion, limbo, the sky-white waters
of the river Lethe. It catches

the morning glories, too, on a trellis of pale dreams, un-

prepared in their
flimsy French dresses with no

underwear. It is

my father trudging home, smelling cool, blue, in June, after
delivering mail all day—a slip, or a comma

of cigarette smoke behind him, lingering
over an old

man's tender, pink
apothecary roses. Breeze

between the cracks

of a garden's brick

forgetful wall. *Here's your bad news, Mrs. Smith. Here's*

a letter from your lost
daughter, Mrs. Jones. Oh

the old women waited all day for the mail, then
hated the mailman when it came. Perhaps

my mother baked
a rhubarb pie

for those old ladies when their husbands died. Remember

how her rhubarbs grew
miraculous in June, massive-

handed, and how that pie would taste
veiny and lush inside, red

velvet and smooth as some un-

domesticated animal's
succulent, clotted blood? It was

like memory itself. A stomach

of sugar, a small red purse. Evening

would come in a gulp. Night poured over our beds
like thick, black glue. Morning flew up on the backs of birds

who pecked the sky to shreds. And afternoon

was nothing. Now

that old Sphinx whispers as it paddles its path across our lawns, *Let*

bygones be

bygones: But

where have we gone?

JOBS

Father

He says, *All jobs are the same*
including God's. Some
break your back, and some
bore you to death.

———————————

Mother

She says, *Once*
I wore another woman's hat home from a dance. It had

a V of lilacs, a cool
spray of cherub breath. Her husband, quite mistaken,
followed me to bed.

———————————

Baker

Even a cake can be made in the shape of a baby. It has
a marzipan bottle, a blue
icing eye, and little
cornstarch flowers
decorate its wrist: *This*

is the sacrifice
a baker has to make

every day of his life: Behind

the bakery's plate glass case, his

baby turns to air—pure as joy, growing stale.

———————————

Child

It thinks, *Something*
has gone rotten

in the heat.   I
smell it beyond the honey-

suckle and over the sweet dust
of roses strangling each other
behind the fence.   It is

the shepherd
growing tired of sheep. He's

feeding them blandly to the jackals
one by one, while the jackals dance themselves
to bread & butter

under a golden sun.

BLACK BEAR PAW $20

For a year my mother felt the phantom breast
beneath her dress   her slip   a bra
molded out in foam to form
the soft lost part for a world
that was also lost
and then she died   And here, a paw

upturned in paper towel.

And my grandmother claimed
the amputated toes were always
ice cold
even in summer   And here

just the paw, still feeling the lost part, dark
mass of itself, massive, missing, and dark

shimmering
its blue-tipped fur in a virgin
forest of sap
and skunk cabbage   muzzling
into June
like a fresh white bed. It rises—

a wide blank space
on hind legs—and sniffs
decayed meat in the air. It remembers

how it lingered in the cherries and the garbage
between the dead
and the doomed   and now, just meat, fat, fur
in an empty cave
in no weather   then

wading into cool water
until it disappears, a breaststroke
and it steps back up
on the black sand

of an opposite shore   with no food

or furniture, rifles, helicopters, friends:
a bear on a chain, the verb *to bear*
as it licks
the trainer's hand, takes
a human husband, nurses
a human child, leaves

one paw print behind
in dried mud
and one paw for the world's
butcher and slaughter to buy

There are four-legged women
There are one-legged women
There are Barnum
& Bailey bears who dance on white-

hot metal plates, fear
and folklore mauling them down to their paws, sweet

and gelatinous, a delicacy, in the warm

musty breath that comes
after everything you long for is gone, and still
you're nosing fallen apples
out of an early snow, voided
and all empty paw.

PRAYERS TO ST. VANITY

My dry well. I beseech thee. This
old lighthouse: Once

it could catch fire
and burn the woman inside alive.

—————————————

In Alpena they'll tell you a lightkeeper's wife
haunts Lake Huron
out of spite. She wails

over the waves. Her ghost
is a gull, a cloud, a rag, a trout
with wings, and gray. They say
the lightkeeper locked her in the light-

house every night, then
went to visit a girl in town. Finally

she burned it down, with herself
inside, alive.

—————————————

St. Vanity, my body
is that burning tower tonight
with that mad wife inside, with that

feverish girl outside
waiting for him in town. Lake

Huron is a blue-black churning
urge to drown, colder
and more filmy
than a tooth.

———————————

The world is spun
by tired giants, younger

women, spite. Now,
that wife grows

older, or she dies. *May*

she not die. Too

many ships have sunk
with trunks of money and all
our mothers' lovers, just

because the light

in that lighthouse was out.

———————————

Love, St. Vanity, is dull
as death by natural causes. It never

sews its own shroud closed: My

dry well, I tell you, when
my husband touches me
my insides are a herd of skinny girls

running backwards, laughing, making
kisses at the sky.

_____

St. Vanity, you know so well
the differences between

the fears of the rich
the fears of the poor

the fears of the beautiful
the fears of the homely

the fears of the young
the fears of the old

the desire to die
and the act of dying

and you cannot bless us all.

SPIRITUS

Jonah in the whale, Jesus
in the tomb, our father asleep in the basement, *TV
Guide* fallen exhausted and open
on an old couch beside him like

a glossy Bible, or a bird

with very weak wings. But one of us

always had a beautiful
pale and drunken mother
who wanted to dance with the girls
in beige stockings until morning, her

toe nails painted white, and
a flat enamel of no
real expression on her face. When

slumber failed, the Mother of God
said to her father the son, *The suburbs
have no decent wine. All
over the Midwest
the teenage girls are drinking* _____. It was

the best miracle of all, one
only a mother could come up with. It was
the feminine devil casting out feminine devils, who leapt

like burning sparrows, burning
rats with wings, burning *Reader's Digests* from
a madwoman's head. Popcorn
gnashed by braces and

Judy Garland scratched at that

blank white blanket of empty bliss that hovered
above our friend's virgin bed, while her mother

smoked Virginia Slims
to ashy pillars. We

looked up to that woman as if
to the hueless future
of our world, her

faded hair dyed black, smile
vacant as lipstick left
overnight on the rim
of a crumpled, styrofoam cup. She

struck a rock in the desert, and it poured forth.

That girl's mother wanted
to be us, and we dreaded
being ourselves, our mothers, our friends so much
we drank more Mogan David that night than a Pharaoh
could drink

in his whole life, un-
bandaged and female
in soggy white light un-
winding from the TV like a mummy

slowly peeled, and revealed, while

some girl's lovely funny awful head-
long sad and drunken mother poled
us to morning on a ferry, dark
and slow against the current, ghost-

white and floating
up the Nile all night, until

the whole herd of us rushed
down the steep bank
into water, drunk

and drowned. Then

Everything we wanted for the rest of our lives was exactly the same
but bathed in rose light

Everything we wanted was exactly the same
but packed in blue-white ice

Everything was the same
but a delicacy, a delicacy, and white

as the cotton that stuffs the virgin
pill bottle's throat: Aspirin and ash and love's

colorless, dry tongue—all of it strung
tight as good faux pearls—lovely
ropes of too-
soft teeth, too

beautiful to eat, two
nooses of glue jewels, phony

as youth and her mother.

CENTURY

Coldest night of the century in a one hundred year old house

One hundred Januarys line up tonight
in the parlor like
sisters dead
from the same disease, wax-white in candlelight

in pine white coffins. *Snow*
the wind howls as it blows.

Pneumonia. A viola. Flute. Cancer. Dance. If those

sisters were here now, I'd tell them how
the Depression will come and go

like an empty, metal bowl. The world

Wars—each
another row of handsome soldiers down the road The heart's

a fist of mud, wet
and warm as a bog, or

a bloody blackbird nest in our chests. A desire

could be preserved
for a century in there. And the sky
is also all

pining and desire—layered
with frozen leaves

and a thatch of sweet decay—*you thought*

you could slip
into a uniform, and sneak away. You thought

melodrama was something
that happened on a stage. Tonight

I want to die
of love, however stupidly, or kill for it, or freeze, or burn, or bleed,

or make you bleed. When I

look outside I see

dead women's dresses etched by my reflection
in every window pane, and hear

the weatherman in the attic drag
his rusty chains
above my bed, pleading

for a woman
who's forgotten she left him there, while

another century of men and weather, of

fingers, knives, and human ice, blows by.

YOUNG MEN IN HEAVEN

A few teeth
in the soft flesh, and the dog
tags, in the green dark

of the body bag. Teeth, and flesh, and tags: Multitude

and solitude
in the green dark quiet, which
has always repeated your name.

———————————

I had to turn away to breathe. The surgeons
were angry with me. I

was studying to be a plumber. It's what

I wanted to be. Mother-

fucker, *someone said,* This plumber's dead.

———————————

Your name shouted
by a crowd, rocketed
into the sky, the confetti, and the lights, and the girls

shaking planets
of shredded paper
and above it, a spinning, uncatchable ball. All

those years, your name inside you, soft

in its shell, like the brain
in the skull, the soul

in the body, imprisoned
like a mollusk. Now

the sky's about to drop,
and your name whistles, silly, as it falls.

You've taken your helmet off.

———————————

The boy did not see the sign
that said STOP. There'd been
a woman at the end
of the road instead. She was

holding the radiant baby
who'd once been him in her arms, and

she simply motioned him on.

———————————

The body behind the garage is happy
to be found.

Its shirt is made of moss.
There is abundance in its mouth.

It crosses its arms to watch

the housewife running back into the house.

———————————

Welcome, the sign above the golf course said.

There was lightning in the distance, a few

friends there to greet him, and a few
old women
he knew were once his aunts. When it

began to drizzle, he stood
beneath a tree, the sky
grew dark. Then

something hot and white dropped
out of it into his hands, and he

held it for a second, like brevity itself, or

the star that bore his name
for a few years in heaven.

Three

——

"I have the white and black girdles, but if I could choose I would get
a lovely shade of lilac . . ."
woman quoted in *Intimate Apparel* magazine

The executioner is, I believe, very expert;
and my neck is very slender.
Anne Boleyn

GRAY LADIES

*"Gray Ladies" is a term for the ghosts of women who
died violently for the sake of love or pined away from
the loss of love.*

Sparrows on our dinner plates, and all
of female heaven's just
a murmur of feeble wings
and dreary weather
beneath a silver dome.

On sunny days we dry our soggy
wings out over England

and it begins rain

and the black currants weep like
blisters on our high-heeled feet.

———————————

That girl over there, she's

pale—an exhalation—a girl

you pass through like Nebraska

on a white-washed day, a girl

not unlike a crystal

bowl of cooled affection, or

evaporated rain.

———————————

She says,

One spring I was Mayqueen
until another girl chased me

out of my youth and down to a dark

stream, where

willows were milling around
like restless men. I

remembered, then, being
young, how

once I'd seen a truck of sheep
all of them dancing to stand
as the truck U-turned in an empty street. That

frantic dignity of sheep, was that me?

———————————

Heaven
is clammy and cool, and for dinner we eat a stew

of moist, gray feathers
and boiled potatoes.

It will be another evening
of dull, parlor games, *Iron*
Maiden, Old Maid—and it always

ends the same. Morning's

just a foggy, naked, female snail
climbing a slippery rock, a phantom
hennery, the cluck
of romance

or the vapor
of invisible, flightless birds.

She wakes one morning as a girl in a billboard

pressed flat and smiling in a one-dimensional sky.

See how she is beautiful with something missing?

One cannot see the foreground

from the background

on a day this bright.

My mother always said, *If tears
were blood*

by now I would be dead
and as my mother said it, something's

tail could be heard in the basement
thumping a hollow wall.

From a gash in the curtains I can see

the MOTEL CACTUS neon
brand the night. There's
something humid and half-human

moving through the desert weeds. She's
carrying a tray of flowered teacups

filled with gray, and her
skirts are epidermal—

wattled, moist, and female
as sentimental rage.

AMAZING COLOSSAL MAN

1956 movie in which a Nevada Test Site worker,
contaminated with radioactive waste, terrorizes Las Vegas.

He is amazing without faith:

Big guy digging a big hole
to poke his face out of the sky.

_____

Divorce is a bouquet
of small explosives

or white roses, the sound

of tin cans dragging
behind a station wagon

like broken chains. It

asks, in the voice of a mechanical child, *Who*

are you? Who are you? And now
how will you ever know?

_____

Amazing Colossal Man grows eight feet a day. He

is greater than his Creator. The birds that fly around his face

are nervous beauty, delicate
sensibilities, blown about
by pure, white wind. They

were human women once, like us.
Once, God walked the Earth in search of love, like him.

—————————————

It was

the spring of '56 when
the girls at the College for Girls
put their dictation down. There was

the sound
of little bird hearts pounding

like feminine machine guns
firing at a crowd.

—————————————

And what did they mean, our vows?

It was a season of high fevers. The sound
of a thousand oboes exploded

from a can of corn when it was opened. Before

the century's over, God

regrets Creation. One
day he says, *Now all the fruit's forbidden*.
But it's too late.

—————————————

My life, a toy life, her husband thinks.

This town, a doom town, his wife says.

_____

A house is built in the desert, furnished

with brand-name foods in the fridge, glass

of water on the nightstand, dummy

husband, mannequin wife, two false kids. Even

the TV's on. Then

the skin of the sky and the atom's split.

End Result of Experiment:

Simulated family blown to bits.

ROXY'S BORDELLO, BOARDED UP

It was never much more than a trailer, a barracks, a row
of old beds and feathered pillows

sunk into night
and memory like

a long boat on a dark ocean, or

a bird in mud. Just

a thin mattress, here and there, a dark-
haired girl with a lisp. The wind

whistles ditties
through its loose teeth, *She*

who has no husband now, will never have one. She
who calls her child

by another child's name
will stand without shoes
a whole life

in a neighborhood of riddles, failure, blame, while

the suburb's daughters sew

Infinity
out of nothing

with thick, red thread. There's

the sound of a sweatshop somewhere, that
dull foot-thump
of murky servant girls working

eternally underground, while the first

night of winter
travels toward us
wondrously cold, dressed

in a gown
of viruses
and phlegm. The whore

who doesn't die
gets old and stands alone
on the deck of a vessel that's circled

with ghost-white birds that beat

a blur of white
gloved hands and gull
black blood. Tonight

her sinking ship is strung
with ornamental lights, or

Christian martyrs' names—their

dim faces
snuffed flames.

SHE SENDS DOWN TOYS FROM THE STARS

She sends down toys from the stars.
Hot, bright, terrible toys—a box

of broken glass, a little wolf on a string, puppets
of frustration

and howling light. She sends

up toys from the sea
with fins and wings and scales like stars
of flaking skin, and he cries
and begs me to make her leave. But

my mother's love has become
a kind of stubbornness that's hushed
as a room without wind since she died. It must

be all those years
in the desert, where they find
the body of a woman

and her child every day, *their*

brown Honda broken down, and two
bored boys with a gun, and she

cannot understand why her grandson will not come

when she opens up her arms, why
he doesn't recognize

her teeth are kind of smile
made of memory and sky. Once

I tried to send
violets to a friend, but the florist
wouldn't even try

to order them. *In Phoenix? In July? They'll*

just dry up and die. So I

sent a plant like panic, full
of barbs and taunts instead. *Thank you*

for the cactus, her note said, *It*
will live forever, but
when I went to visit

there was no cactus there.

WARNING:

Here they've hacked some
poor smoker into steaks
and made us a slide-
show of his lungs. The tile

in the bathroom
of the community college
is cold, and there's

a chaos of faces before I faint
and the dull bell of my head on the floor
summons the smoking

dead from their graves, the rumpled
lungs of my uncles, the creamy
corpse-eyes of my friends

and the earth falls apart like dirt
as I try to hold my own
crumbling chest
together. A girl

has run to get my husband
who is having a cigarette outside.
We have to quit I tell him
on the car ride home

and I show him the message
from the Surgeon General
as I smack the last one
out of the pack.

The first day passes so slow
we can feel our hair
grow, even
under our arms, our eye-
lashes even. Then

the elementary school
where we were students burns
to the ground, just
some rags left flapping
on the flag-pole, nostrils

and ashes, steaming
volcanoes, and the message
a dead bird brings us
as it falls at our feet
in a soggy ball. Before

we go to bed I rip
my underwear off. Someone
has poisoned my black bra
and my torso has turned

to roast beef. I hear
my husband grind his teeth
all night in sleep

and in the morning
he rolls over in bed
to smile at me
and the teeth are gone, just

a bloody smithereen left
hanging from his gums, a molar
on his pillow. We

choose our plots that same day
at the Catholic ceme-
tery—two
together just beyond

the chain-link fence, where
the suicides are buried
beside the musicians.

WEATHER

The planet is harmless. It rises
with weather and buoys, a cool
blue satellite strung
with cobwebs to the moon. The way

my richest high school boyfriend used to blow
his condoms into dim balloons
and bat them above the bed like
bald men with beige
stockings on their heads. Those

men robbed banks every day
and no one remembered a thing. Just
the weather that December and the way
the weather vane screamed
with rust when it was spun. Just

shock's sweet narcotic, juice
clear as gin
squeezed from a small dry stone. When

it snows up here they say that God
is beating his angels again, or
the farmer's wife in heaven
is plucking her white hen. If

those condoms didn't deflate, they'd
explode in someone's face: Twice
that boyfriend put his fist
through the drywall behind my bed. Stoned,

the headlights fell and rose
like UFO's or saints, like

ghost gloves in the bedroom dusting
his blank face, in

the middle of the night, in
the big dumb dark.   Some-
where, a needle flashed and spun

like a moth's bright spine
in a nurse's glove, *the moist*

fog of an old
woman's lung, the low

rumble of something done.   I loved

every rich boy who touched me
after I loved that one.   And though

I can't recall his face, I never forgot the way
the buckle of his belt stuck
cold in my stomach as a mugger's

smudged gun when we hugged, or how

the weather was always
drenched as a sweater, all
tenderness and a soggy

paper sack of nails, *bloody*
blood and rust: In those
days, love

was cheap and small, a pink
plastic item, and any girl could buy it

or steal it at the mall.

WHERE ARE THESE CHILD STARS NOW?

There are faces inside the faces
of these child stars grown old. Cherubs,
and babies, who make
a caricature of pain and addiction as I page. I feel

a cold flame on the tip
of my tongue, and see

a woman searching for her lost tooth
in a bucket of blood, and on

every radio station I hear
their voices for the rest of the day, voices

which advertise cruises, now

that they are only voices—voices
in luminous sweaters. Voices
floating loosely inside
sleeves of thread and light, holding
glasses and decanters
in their voices' hands. White

and slippery shoes
on their voices' feet, while
the sun on the water gleams like a spoonful of diamonds

force-fed to a child. There is
delicate vegetation
on the islands of which they speak.

Pink orchards of fruit singing.
Flowers that dance like fancy hats.

But the sea makes a sound
like the slaughter of animals
drowning their voices out.

SAD SONG

There are women
carrying torches
coming toward us. Their

eyes are accidents. The kind
that happen on the highway
in the middle of the night. The kind

we glimpse as we drive by. A flare
in snow, a metal cage
with ruined tigers in it. We
look away, and then we're home. There

are hundreds of women marching forward, carrying
torches like a burning orchard. They're
coming for us, and everything's on fire. Even

the torpedo boats. Even the starfish creeping along
the ocean floor in families, in

the utterly deaf and dumb. Here

they come: You
open your mouth and I
see the word *bye*
float out, like
a jeweled wasp with

a golden Y around her neck. Those

wasps have made
an elaborate nest in the attic, in

my trunk of party dresses: All
that buzzing about you, all
that frantic dancing

like a barbed breeze in my hair. I

lift the lid of that trunk
for the first time in years. Stale

carnations and yellow lace. All
the invitations I didn't take
turned to female dust. *I'll*

always love you I say, and you
wince a bit like Zeus
who didn't know he had

an armored woman in his head. Those

women wait
with their torches on the porch, but when
I step outside to take
my own flaming place, they

turn suddenly to stone, like
all the marble madonnas, trapped
and standing
on Saturday

at the empty art museum. Their

long medieval shadows drape the floor like
loose blue cloaks: Look

carefully under the veil
of one of those—the one
who has been waiting at his tomb
for seven hundred years. If

you hold your breath you'll see
she's grieving

with a sly, white smile. Perhaps
that one's only posing

as a stone. Maybe

she's just as alive as the garden hose, coiled
and breathing in the dank
dark of the garden shed. Perhaps

she's held her stone breath
a long, long time: The way
some moths, fearing nets, will

fold their wings in half
and seem to the untrained eye to be
just a few more brown and withered leaves

clinging to the tree. But

they're not: If

you sing a sad song loud enough, the boys
on those torpedo boats
can hear you under the sea.

NIGHT

There are the plaster stars, the dew's

slow mucilage
in the garden, and God

spreads himself across the heavens

without form. All

that smeared star froth pads
the moon in cotton, a doughy

opal, a Peeping Tom's
featureless face at the window

glowing, while

shed bandages of fog, bacterial
and womanish, rise
from the lawn

when she takes her girdle off.